Notalie natters about what matters

Notalie Knot

Pizzazz

First published in 2012

Published by Pizzazz Limited
1 The Three Horseshoes, Somerton Road,
Upper Heyford, Oxon OX25 1JU

books@pizzazz.eu

ISBN: 978-0-9573730-1-3

Book set in Book Antiqua
and designed by Judy Whiteside

Printed and bound in Great Britain

For my Mum

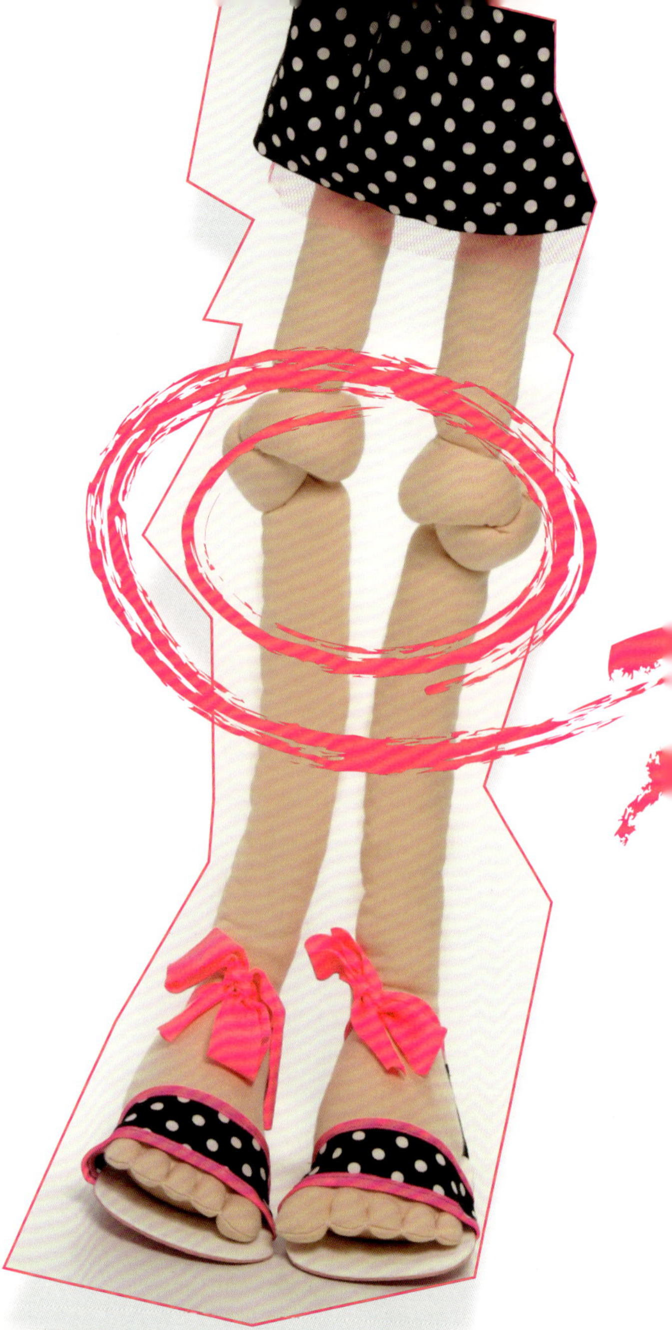

Natter-knickers !!!

That's what my Mum calls me. It's her way of saying that I talk too much, but I don't think I do talk too much. My mouth is just saying what's in my brain!

She also says I've got legs like knotted string...... thanks Mum, that's soooo flattering!

Hi! I'm Notalie, but most of my friends and family call me 'Nots', because I've got knotty knees.

In fact I'm pretty funny looking, but I just love that because it makes me different. I am my own person with my very own style.

I'm loving...

My best friends... my style... staying stretchy... making stuff ...giving pressies... sleepovers... ...chocolate... my world... my dog, Hitch... notebooks and pencils..... spotty-dotty things... making up my own special words...... but, most of all, being me!

This is ME at a sleepover at Bim's house

Stop shouting!

I'm loving...

not...

Bullies...

meanies...

too much homework...

shouty people

on mobiles...

...tidying my room....

cricket on the TV.... and

my big sister

when she's

scrinchy!

Does THIS look untidy to you?!

I'm growing up and it's making me do a lot of thinking. My world sometimes makes my head 'fuzz'...it's sooo confusing.

'Grups' are always telling me what to do, but most of the time they say one thing and do something completely different.

Like my Dad nags me about watching too much TV and then spends three zillion hours, boggled-eyed watching totally yawny cricket. If I complain he just says, "You do as I say, not as I do, young lady!"

He only calls me 'Young Lady' when he's 'scrinchy'.

So now, I'm putting on my 'thinking cap' and 'thinking face' too!

I'm trying to un-muddle stuff in my brain and make up my own mind. I think that's best.

Sometimes people think I look really bored, but I'm not. It just means that my head is busy and I'm concentrating on my 'thinkings'.

Today I'm thinking about all the people in my life. Most are lovely, like my family and my very best friends, but some are not so nice, like bullies and meanies.

I'm loving my family loads. Mum, Dad, Gran and even my totally 'irribabble' sister Scattie Tattie.

We are a bigly boringly, normal family and I suppose that's a good thing, but I sometimes wish I could swap Scattie for a nicer sister. You just get your family 'cos you're born in them, but with your 'besties' you get to choose!

My 'besties' are all very different girls, but when you put them all together they make an awesome thing................ it's called friendship.

I like to know what words mean, so I looked up the word 'friendship' in Dad's big word book, the dictionary. It's a bit 'posh-speak' but it says...

Friendship *n.* relationship of mutual affection and good will.

In 'my-speak' that means....

FRIENDS
LOVING EACH
OTHER
TO BITS
AND HAVING
A GOOD TIME!"

Why can't the dictionary just say that?

Talking of words, I just love making up my own and when I do I call it

'Notalees'.

That's a new language that I'm creating myself. Look at my Notalees dictionary at the back of the book.

So who are my 'besties'? Well there are six of us and we call ourselves...

The Notstars

The 'Not' bit comes from my name, 'cos I'm the eldest and the tallest and 'stars' because we all twinkle in our own way.

First there's Bimini Skipper, my absolute best friend. She and I are extra close and I can talk to her about anything, even share my biggest secrets and know that she will keep them safe.

She is always there when I need her and never gets scratchy with me, even when I'm whinging about my horrible older sister, Scattie Tattie!

Bim is black, with amazing hair. I call her 'Bimini Butterfly', because her most fave things in the world are...............

.....butterflies!

She has this cool bedroom, all blue and fluttery. She always chooses clothes with butterflies on them and she even has a pair of blue wings. I wish she wouldn't wear them out with me it makes me squirmy with embarrassment. But sometimes I think she will just fly away!

Next is Pearl Parbuckle, she has an awesome idea to get a Notstars netball team together. It's fab because it will help us all to stay stretchy. Her Mum and Dad are totally into fitness, so the whole family do things like go on walking holidays.

I'm thinking it's **really great** for global warming.

No carbon footprints just muddy ones!!

Ditti Hahoy is totally different from me. She's practical and loves maths and scientific stuff. My brain just goes to jelly when I think of maths! She's Asian and comes from a very clever family. They're a bit 'swotty' really, but her Mum makes the best curries!!

Togs Fairway can be a bit of a 'bossy-bottom', but she's great at getting things done while the rest of us dither and dawdle. I suppose we need someone like her, because without her nothing would ever get done.

Then there's Phoebe Beaufort. Isn't Phoebe a funny spelling? It's pronounced Feebee, so we just call her Feebs. She's very musical, plays the flute and sings in the school choir. Some 'idiwits' at school call her 'flakey', but they are just being mean and stupid.

She reminds me of an angel, all floaty and calm.

Feebs does not do stress!

Then there's the tiniest member of the Notstars. He's my lazy dog, **Hitch**. I totally love him and we are the best of friends. He comes to all our sleepovers and enjoys getting fussed by the girls.

So here we are, the Notstars. Just about the coolest group of friends any girl could have, but there's always room for more girls like us. Girls who are brave, funny, full of 'fabaroonie' ideas and who want to be good friends.

Me and my friends are all so different and we're not always sugary-sweet to each other. Sometimes we really argue and get 'splodie', but we soon make up and we love each other just the same.

Bimini
Pearl
Ditti

Togs
Phoebe
Hitch!

When I've got my **thinking face** on, I like to make a list. It helps me to un-knottle my **'thinkings'** and that's **really** important. So, this is my list about friends...

What is a friend?

1. Someone who likes your good bits, but understands your bad bits too and loves you for them both.

2. A person who doesn't care if you are tall, short, skinny, round, pink, black, brown.......... or spotty!

3. The person you have absolutely THE MOST FUN with.

4. The one who makes you feel good about yourself and expects nothing in return.

5. Someone who stays your friend in the smelly times as well as the happy ones.

That's **my** list, but what would yours be? What do you think about **your** friends?

Sometimes, when we all get together I think that **we're like a big pizza!**

Like we're all the different toppings that mix up to make a disc of deliciousness!

Pizza without toppings would be booooring and life without the Notstars would be just the same.

So what toppings would we be?

First, Bimini. That's easy. It's soooo got to be the **melty cheese**, because that's my absolute favourite bit!

Next, Pearl ~ because she's sporty, she could be the **tomato** ~ the healthy bit. And she always has a red, 'splodie' face when she's been running.

Ditti's Mum makes the most exotic curries, so she will have to be the hot and spicy bit.......... **pepperoni**.

Togs is a bit bossy, so I'm thinking she wouldn't want to be on the Pizza, she would want to make it! So she would have to be the chef.

Feebs is so floaty, she would have to be the tiny, herby bits that get sprinkled on the top.

Ooops, I nearly forgot Hitch. When it comes to pizza, he just wants to eat it!

What about moi! I would be the pizza base, because it's my job to hold the Notstars together. I love that and I always share my thinkings with the girls, just like we share our pizza.

I love that we are all individuals, but when we mix all our talents together, the result is simply delicious!

That's my

Notstars Pizza.

But, what would yours be? Think about your friends and see what kind of **pizza** they would make.

What kind of toppings would YOUR friends be?

Scribble your ideas in the pizza slices

I'm going to have to stop thinking about this now, because I'm getting starving hungry. Mmm, I just had a brill idea ....chocolate pizza!

Sometimes I imagine how it would be if I didn't have my funny, 'fabolistic' friends. I'm thinking that it would feel like being really cold all the time. My best friends are like a big, soft, snuggy duvet that keeps me safe and warm.

I think it's totally amazing, because we all have such different characters, but we really are all stars and shine in our own ways.

We've put our brains together and created our own 'Notstars Promise'. We always read this aloud whenever we all get together. Some girls may think it's a pathetic idea, but it really helps us stay focussed on how to be best friends.

The Notstars Promise

Friends should.......

Stay friends in good times... and bad ones, too.

Promise to listen to each other's point of view.

Always work together as a team.

Remember birthdays.

Keep each other's secrets.

Laugh out loud together,

Iron out arguments before it's too late.

Never forget to share their dreams.

Give lots of hugs when they are needed.

Never be mean to one another.

Offer friendship to new friends too.

Tell each other the truth.

Share their choccies.

Trust each other.

Always help each other.

Respect one another.

Share their fashion passion.

Can you see what
it spells out?

Sparkling Notstars

Now try this with your friends and see what your promise will be.

This is my
happy face... NOT!!!

Unhappy birthday!

Everything is totally fluffy when friends are fine and there are no problems, but sometimes things go wrong and you have to be a very good friend to make things better. It happened to me last year… and it was my **birthday**! This is what happened...

"Happy birthday to you..." Mum was singing from the kitchen

but I WAS NOT **HAPPY**!!

This was my most absolutely special, very own day of the whole year, so why did I have to go to school?

No one should go to school on their birthday. Everyone should take a holiday, a day to do what they want to do!

Eventually I slid out of bed and into my school uniform. Mum was flapping because I was late. I didn't even have time to open my birthday presents.

We started the walk to school. Actually it was more like stomping. Usually I'm quite bounciful when I go to school, but that day my footsteps were 'clompy'!

Mum was chirpy and twittering away about my birthday cake, but I wasn't interested. I was in a mood.

Clomping makes you slow and we were really late, so we had to speed-walk the rest of the way. I couldn't be late because Mrs Killick was on duty at the gate.

We call her 'Scary Mary from the dairy!' She's totally strict, so I didn't want one of her 'What time do you call this?' looks.

I kissed Mum goodbye and scooted into the playground, where the Notstars where waiting for me. They all burst out singing a very loud and embarrassing version of Happy Birthday to you!

"Happy birthday to you
No one looks like you do
Your legs are like knotted string
And your feet smell like poo!!!"

They were just being total 'idiwits', so I just laughed. They are my very best of besties BUT, I want you to know that my feet absolutely DO NOT SMELL OF POO!

Togs gave me my first pressie, a 'fabaroonie' notebook in the shape of a shoe. I'm loving notebooks and shoes are my absolute passion. I've got 23 notebooks but nowhere near enough shoes.

Ditti gave me a gorgeous, pink beady bracelet with stars. Pearl chose a spotty, sporty headband for me to wear when I get st-r-e-t–c–h-y and work out.

Feeb's pressie was a sweet little bell that tinkles when you hold it in the breeze.

Then I realised that something was odd… no Bimini! Where was she? She would never miss my birthday and always made me a divine pressie.

"Where's Bimini?" I asked. The Notstars just stared at their feet. Then Pearl pointed across the playground.

"She's over there by the wall, but she's not talking to us."

I turned and ran towards Bim, but as soon as she saw me she hurried away and disappeared into the school . She avoided me all day.

I just wanted school to be over. My tum did flip-flops all day and I wanted to be sick.

Mum came to meet me and we walked through the crowds. They were giggly and excited, but I felt like I was the loneliest girl in the entire world.

I didn't really want to talk, but Mum was still being chirpy and she asked, "Good day at school, my special Birthday Princess?"

She had **no idea**! My birthday had been

TOTAL

POOEY

PANTS!!

I just grunted and tried to smile, but my lips just 'wibbled'.

When we got home Mum took the lid off the big pink cake tin and started to press curly swirls of chocolate into the thick, gooey icing on the top of the perfect 'Chocco Heaven' birthday cake.

Mum knows my birthday cake MUST be chocolate.

I couldn't hold it in any longer, so I told her about Bimini. She simply cut a big slice of squidgy birthday cake and smiled.

"Come on Birthday Princess. Eat your cake and it will be fine."

I didn't want to be mean to Mum, but really.... it was going to take much more than cake to make things fluffy again.

I pretended to enjoy my birthday tea and even Scattie Tattie was trying to be nice. Mum's cake was 'superbulously' delicious

but I still felt totally miserable.

How could my best friend be so mean to me?

Normally chocolate cake will cure anything, but my insides just felt like lumpy custard and stingy tears started to dribble from my eyes. Mum pulled out a tissue and held it to my nose.

"Blow hard. You can't have a runny nose on your birthday, it's so unattractive!"

I blew and tried to make a little smile. "That's better." said Mum. "There will be a perfectly simple explanation, I'll ring her Mum right now and find out what's wrong. This isn't like Bimini at all."

I stayed in the kitchen and pushed the gooey chocolate cake crumbs round my plate. I could hear Mum talking on the phone.

"Oh, I'm so sorry, so sorry."
Then a long silence, followed by another.
"Oh, I'm so sorry." Silence...............
"Oh, my dear."
...........Silence............ "Is there anything I can do to help?"

Now I was really worried, it sounded serious. Mum came back into the kitchen shaking her head and looking very sad.

"That explains it." She sat down, took my hand and held it tight. "Bimini's Mum and Dad have split up and her Dad has moved out of the flat. She's finding it really hard to tell anyone ~ even you, and you are her very best friend."

Poor Bim! All this time I had just been thinking about ME, ME, ME. I never once thought that Bimini might have a problem. I tried to imagine how I would feel if my Mum and Dad had split.

I know Dad can be 'scrinchy' sometimes, but I love him and I'd really miss him.

Bimini needed help ~ my help. It wasn't about me at all. I had been soooo selfish. Then I remembered our

Notstars Promise...

Best friends should stay friends in GOOD times... and bad times TOO!

I knew exactly what I had to do. I cut the biggest slice of birthday cake and carefully wrapped it in foil.

"Mum, please can we go to Bim's?" I asked and pushed the cake into my pocket. There was no time to lose.

"No probs." Smiled Mum. "I'll get my coat right now."

This time we almost ran down the High Street, past Curry Nights, the new Indian Restaurant where Mr Patel was busy setting the tables for his evening customers. Then round the corner at last, into Bimini's road.

She lives in a flat in a big Victorian house. By the time we got there, I was **totally gaspy**, out of breath and my face looked 'splodie'.

I ran up the steps and rang the bell by the big front door. It was ages before Bim opened it and, when she saw it was me, she burst into tears and threw her arms around my neck.

She hugged me so tightly I could feel the chocolate cake squidging between us!

Her shoulders wobbled because she was sobbing so hard. I was beginning to get a bit soggy from her tears, but I gave her the biggest hug I could manage and held on till my arms started to 'twingle'.

Her Mum, Mrs Skipper, came out of the kitchen and looked very sad, so I ran over to her and gave her a hug too. She smiled.

"OK, enough blubbing now! I think you two should go to Bimini's room and have a good old chat. I'll bring you some mango juice."

Our Mums went into the kitchen for a chat too and we flopped on the saggy, old bean bag in the middle of Bim's room.

She told me the whole story about her Mum and Dad. They had argued a lot and this time they weren't going to make up. So her Dad had decided it would be better if he went to live somewhere else.

It made Bim very sad because she loves them both. She'll still see lots of her Dad and he loves her lots, but it's not quite the same as having him at home.

After a while Bim's Mum came in and and smiled. "I'm glad you two are talking again.

"When things get bad, good friends make things better."

I handed Bimini the crumbled cake. "It's a bit squished and gooey, but it's still Chocco Heaven."

We shared the crumbly mess and soon we were laughing like we always do.

When it was time to go home, Bim opened the drawer in her bedside cabinet and brought out a little parcel. "It's for you... Happy,

Happy Birthday!

Sorry it's bit late."

I undid the little blue ribbon and it fell to the floor. Inside the scrunchy wrapping paper was a sweet little purse with a butterfly stitched on the side.

"I made it especially for you," she said. "I thought it would look brill with your new bag."

I wanted to blub again, but I was all **blubbed-out**! It was so beautiful and she had made it just for me. I thanked her and we had one more, **squeezy** hug.

I felt warm inside and I skipped home, my hand in Mum's.

By now Curry Nights was full of noisy people tucking into to poppadums and Passanda. I felt so bouncy I waved to them as I passed by.

In bed that night I thought hard about the day. It made me think that sometimes things aren't always the way they look.

I had just thought about Moi, Moi, Moi and I promised myself I would try a lot harder to be a 'superbulous' 'bestie' to all my friends.

I need to be **extra watchy**, so I know when my friends need help.

I think I'd better get more choccies too ~ I've a feeling I might need them!

Chocolate helps make most things better!

That weekend Mum and Dad took me to Pizzamucho, my favourite eating place. I invited all the Notstars for a belated Birthday Bash. We laughed so much I think we were the loudest table there.

Togs did her 'Mrs Killick' impersonation and we were all in stitches.

I realised just how lucky we were to be friends. Bimini was back and it was as if nothing bad would ever happen again. I know things can't always be perfect, but with good friends we can make things right again.

Chocolate to the rescue!

A chocolate in the hand is worth two in the shop!

That's one of my special sayings. You can depend on chocolate. Even when Mum is being totally **'splodie'** at me 'cos my room is in a mess or when my homework is so hard my brain gets knottled!

Velvety, glossy, chocolate **'unknottles'** my brain and makes me springy again.

Have you guessed that I like chocolate? Actually... that's not quite true.

I am absolutely, completely and rapturously, loving it!

I know that if you eat **too** much, your face can get covered in spotty **volcanoes** and your stomach can grow to the size of an Easter egg, but my pocket money is so pathetically **stingy**, I can't **afford** to buy enough to get fat anyway.

I think chocolate helps to make most things better, that's why I like **to share** it with my friends. Sharing your choccies is the best. I always get a warm flutter in my middle when I'm giving a present to someone.

Unless it's to Scattie Tattie, my **'irribabble'** big sister.

She doesn't deserve any chocolate unless it's a chocolate-covered slug or something equally slimy!

Chocolate makes a fab present for friends. Not just buying a box from the shop, but making stuff yourself.

I always make presents for my best friends because it makes them special.

But don't forget to ask Mum to help! Mums get very 'splodie' if you mess up their kitchens and you must have their help with the cooking bit.

These are my 'scrumerooniest' recipes....

on the next page......

Chocolate Wodge

This is sooooo easy to make, and **very** easy to eat so make sure you leave plenty for your friends.

You will need...

225 gms digestive biscuits
115 gms butter
1 tablespoon Golden Syrup
2 tablespoons drinking chocolate
1 desertspoon sugar

How to make it...

1 Put the **biscuits** in a plastic bag and bash them with a rolling pin until they are in little pieces. (This is **SOOOO** much fun, but try not to be too noisy.)

2 Put the butter in a saucepan and heat it on the hob till it melts. Then add the sugar, syrup and **drinking chocolate** and stir it all up together.

3 Take the pan off the heat and stir in the crushed up biscuits. Then put the mixture into a shallow tin and smooth it all out.

4 Melt half a large bar of chocolate in the microwave. Spread the melted chocolate all over the top of the mixture in the tin and then put in the fridge to chill.

5 When it's cold cut it into little squares.

6 Cut a big circle of pretty paper. Pop pieces of chocolate wodge in the middle and scrunch the paper around it.

Tie it with a funky bow to make the perfect pressie.

Chocolatti Dip

This is the healthy recipe because you need fruit too!

You will need...

250g good dark chocolate
500ml extra thick cream

What to do next...

1 Pour the cream into a glass bowl and microwave on a medium setting until small bubbles appear.

2 Break up the chocolate into small pieces and add to the cream. Whisk them together until all the chocolate has melted.

3 Pour the mixture into a pretty serving bowl and put in the fridge for about two hours.

4 Then the **fun** really begins. You can dip strawberries, slices of apple , little biscuits……… whatever you can think of. It's also fab if you warm it up a little and pour over ice cream!

Everyone has their **absolute** most favourite 'chocadoobry' and if I ever have my **own** chocolate shop, I'm going to stuff it full of my very favourites and call it

Natalie's ChocoWorld

Imagine spending **every** day in a shop just stuffed with chocs…..

heavenly!

Starry Night

Fashion is my passion, but my own style. I'm not a copy-cat!

I think the most 'fasholicious' night in the world is the Oscars night. I just love watching it on TV. It's the night when they give out prizes to the best actors and all the celebs show off their fashions on a red carpet. (I wonder why it has to be red?)

I love all the 'glamour-puss' dresses and shoes so high my Mum would **never** let me wear them!

You are invited to the **Notscars...**

One night we were at Feeb's house, watching TV. All the stars were arriving for the Oscar awards. They are totally showy-offy, but I just love the floaty, fabulous fashions.

Suddenly Togs had a brainwave! "Let's have our very own awards night. We could call it 'The Notscars'!!

Trust her to come up with a totally awesome idea. Sometimes she makes me want to scream because she can be a bit bossy, but I had to admit this was inspired!

Tog's Mum, Mrs Fairway, said we could all meet at her house. She's very kind and even found an old piece of red carpet. There were loads of things to do, but the most important thing was ~

what to **wear?**

We all decided to keep our 'Notscars look' a secret from one another, so it would be a huge **surprise** on the night.

I just had to do BLING, because

I love to sparkle

Mum let me explore her jewellery box and I found my bridesmaid's tiara that I had to wear at my stupid cousin's wedding...... **too embarrassing!!**

Bim was brill and made a fabulous award in the shape of a golden 'N'. She is just THE BEST when it comes to making stuff.

But the most difficult thing was deciding what the awards would be. We couldn't have Best Actor or anything like that, so we really had to put our thinking caps on.

At last, the special night arrived and we were all bubbling with excitement.

Mum was really helpful and made me a cool dress from an old one of hers. It was very purple with zillions of little sparkles all over it. I'm being a bit boasty, but I did look totally chic in my tiara and bling.

mwah!!

mwah!!

Notalie,
Fashion Diva!
That's moi!

'Dad's Cabs' dropped me off at Togs and I rang the doorbell. The door opened and I got the biggest surprise. There was her Mum wearing a posh dress and dingle-dangle earrings.

"Come this way, Madam," she smiled.

I walked carefully up the stairs to Tog's room, because my tiara was a bit wobbly.

It was awesome! The red carpet stretched from the door to a coffee table which had become our stage. The bendy lamp which normally sits on Tog's desk had become a spotlight and the other lamps were covered in delicate fabric, making pools of coloured light.

Fanmatastical!!!

Bimini was already there, and guess what? She was wearing a blue dress with floaty sleeves like wings and a big **butterfly** pinned in her hair. Her Mum had been busy sewing too.

Togs likes to look 'understated', but she looked **dramatic** in black with bright pink accessories to add a flash of colour.

Next to arrive was Ditti wearing a fabulous silky Churida. It was like a very special dress, but with skinny trousers underneath. Gold bangles jingle-jangled on her wrists and a beautiful bindi sparkled on her forehead.

She looked like an Eastern Princess.

A few minutes later, Pearl made her entrance wearing her usual sporty shorts. Underneath she wore a pair of spotty-dotty socks and completed the look with a funky pea-green top. She looked amazing, but I couldn't help thinking there was something really odd about her.

Then I looked closer.

Sticking out from behind her feet was a pair of fluffy ears!

Then suddenly a small face peered slowly round her shoulder.

It was Feebs!!!

"Hello," she whispered, as she stepped out from behind Pearl.

Everyone gasped and then collapsed into fits of giggles. She was wearing her PJs, dressing gown and bunny slippers!!!

"You are totally 'looperama'!" roared Togs, trying hard to control her giggles. "Who goes to the Oscars in their PJs?"

"Ooops, I totally forgot." Feebs muttered through her embarrassment. "I just thought it was a normal sleepover. Sorry, I'm a total 'idiwit'."

We all stopped laughing. She is so lovely you just can't laugh at her for long.

Ditti gave her a big hug. "Maybe it will become the latest 'Fash-pash'. Bet all the celebs will be wearing PJs next year!"

Just then, Mrs Fairway appeared with a tray full of 'scrumerooni' nibbles and amazing pink drinks that fizzed like real champagne. The bubbles tickled our noses.

We lifted our glasses, clinked them together and made a toast.

To friendship, fashion and the Notstars

Then the ceremony really began. Each one of us, even Feebs, walked the walk along the red carpet and twirled in front of the spotlight. Everyone cheered and pretended to snap loads of photos, just like we were celeb photographers.

When the time came for the awards, Tog's Mum stepped into the spotlight and started her speech.

"Welcome to this glittering occasion. The very first Notscars night!

The competition has been tough and the judging very difficult, but at last we have reached our decision. So without delay.................."

Suddenly my tummy felt all fluttery. What if I didn't win anything? I would totally shrivel up with embarrassment!

She continued... "In the category for 'Very Best Bestie'
the winner is............"

We all held our breath. "Bimini!"

The applause was deafening and we clapped till our hands were stinging.

Bim looked soooo shocked, but eventually she walked along the carpet to accept her prize ~ a chocolate medal wrapped in gold foil.

Thank goodness she didn't make a weepy speech like the real celebs do! Why do they blub and thank everyone in the world? It's just soooooo cringey!

One by one the awards were announced.

★ The 'Miss Fix It' award........... Ditti

★ The 'Total Team Leader' award............. Pearl

★ The 'Miss Make It Happen' award......... Togs

★ The 'Most Original Outfit' award...........Feebs

The cheering continued, but I just felt sick! I wasn't going to get anything. I knew it. Tears started to sting in my eyes.

Then I heard, "Last, but by no means least. The award for 'The Queen of Bling' goes to.......... Notalie!'

Everyone clapped as I went to collect my award.

When the applause finished Mrs Fairway clapped her hands loudly and said, "Now we come to the main award of the evening, The Notstars Trophy.

"This is awarded to the most outstanding girl in the Notstars."

In all the excitement, I had completely forgotten all about this. My tum started to flip-flop again.

The room fell silent and we all looked towards Tog's Mum...

After a few moments she held up the trophy and smiled. "The judges have decided that this magnificent trophy should be awarded to.....................

The Notstars!

"You are ALL fabulous and you are all winners."

We passed the gleaming gold trophy from one to another and cheered at the very top of our voices.

It had been a magical night and Tog's Mum has been a star too, so we gave her three loud 'Hussahs' to say "Thank you."

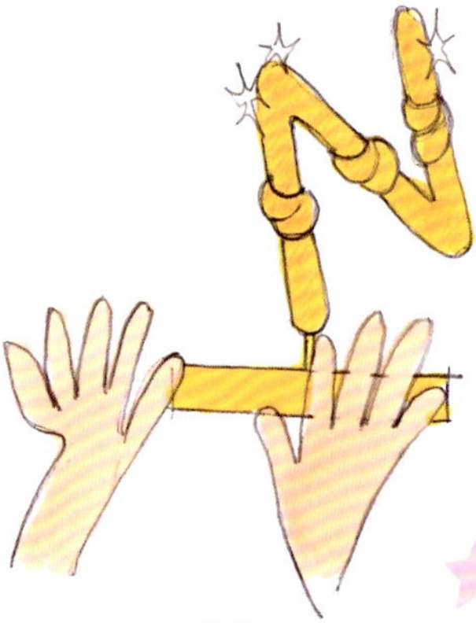

Hussah! Hussah!! Hussah!

Then she left us alone to enjoy our party. We munched up all the nibbles and sipped the rest of our fizz.

We decided to take it in turns to take the trophy home until the next Notscars Night. Togs took the first turn.

Later on, when we felt sleepy, we took off our fashion chic and put on our PJs. This time it was Feeb's turn to laugh at us, because she had been in hers all evening!

One by one, my friends fell into a dreamy sleep, but I lay awake for ages and thought about our glittering night and how special it had been.

I looked around the room at everyone snoozing in their sleeping bags or tucked up in duvets. Over in the corner I could see the Notscars Trophy shining in a moonbeam.

The knot makes us stronger

We wear our special hearts to show that we are loving friends

A warm glow started at my toes and settled in my tummy.

I thought how super lucky I was to be part of such a fabulous knot of friends.

We all won our own prizes because we are special individuals, but we won the trophy because we are together.

I thought about the big celebs in Hollywood and wondered if they had fab friends like mine. Somehow, I don't think they have so much fun. I bet they just meet on red carpets from time to time and that's soooo sad because everyone needs their friends.

I wouldn't swap the Notstars for all the bling in the world!

Natalie

Topsy Turvy

This pic isn't upside down! It's me doing one of my most fave things. I love doing this 'cos it gives me a **topsy-turvy view** of the world.

It helps me think better. Mum says it's because all the blood rushes to my brain. I think she must be right because if I stay like it for too long, I get dizzy!

I'm thinking that having a different view from someone else doesn't mean you are always right.

Like my friend Pearl Parbuckle. She's the most sporty girl I know and she makes sure we all stay healthy.

Sometimes I just want to be a lazy-boots but Pearl encourages us to keep moving and I definitely feel more stretchy when I work out.

She had a 'fabaroonie' idea that we could be a netball team. We're not very good, but we do try hard. We love to bounce the ball around and shoot it over her Mum's washing line (when there's no washing on it, of course). It's really good 'cos it makes you run and jump a lot.

We were just having fun playing the game until Pearl decided to take it very seriously. She announced that we needed our own special kit and would be called 'Pearl's Girlz'... Aaaagh, cringey!

She's not normally bossy, that's Togs's job, but that day she was **horrible**!

Ditti spoke up. "I don't agree, you don't own us, so why do we have to use **your** name?"

"Yes," piped up Togs. "If we use any name it should be The Notstars."

"No way!" said Pearl, who was looking a bit 'splodie' now.

"We've used Notalie's name already and we are **not using it again**."

I kept quiet.

Feebs stepped forward. "Come on let's not be 'scrinchy' with each other.

We're friends.

Maybe we should talk about our kit first. What colour would be nice?"

Feebs is so sweet, she always tries to keep things peaceful.

Pearl was still being shouty.

"I want red!"

"Wouldn't butterfly blue be prettier?" suggested Bimini, politely.

"Actually, I love sunflower yellow," interrupted Ditti. "What about you, Nots?"

It was my turn to speak. "Well, my fave is absolutely pink. How about that?"

"Absolutely not!" Pearl was really cross. 'It needs to be red!'

"Just like your face!" sneered Togs.

The whole situation was really getting out of hand, when suddenly Feeb's little squeaky voice rose above all the others.

"Girls! We're friends, please stop being 'scrinchy'. It's horrible. Let's work together, like we always do. Then we can create something wonderful."

She was right of course. We all went quiet and stared at the ground.

Mrs Parbuckle had heard the kerfuffle and came into the garden to see what all the fuss was about.

"Girls! You sound very cross and that's not like you."

Pearl pushed forward. "It's not fair, Mum. It was my idea, so I get to choose!"

"Choose what?" asked Mrs Parbuckle.

Feebs quietly explained the problem. Pearl's idea was fab, but if we were going to be a team, **we should listen to what each other has to say.**

Pearl's Mum smiled. "I think I have a suggestion. You all like different colours, so why not put them all together and make a rainbow?"

Brilliant!! We all agreed. That was it, everyone loves rainbows. It was the perfect solution for everyone.

"OK, now we just need the name," said Mrs Parbuckle.

It all went very quiet, then Feebs jumped with excitement.

"How about, **'The Rainbows'**?"

"Awesome!!" We all cheered together. "We'll be 'The Rainbows'."

Suddenly I had an idea. "I think we should make Pearl our captain. It was her idea and she is our 'sportsmeister'."

Everyone agreed and that's how 'The Rainbows' started.

Although we're not amazing at netball, we just love having fun together and that's THE BEST!

I'm thinking it's pretty cool that everyone sees things in different ways. It makes the world more interesting.

It's OK not to agree with someone 'cos you see things differently, but it's important to listen to what they have to say too.

If you want to try this upside-down thing, don't do it for too long or you'll dizzy-up yourself... and make sure there's something soft and squidgy under your head!

What would you have on your team T-shirt?

I ♥ Hitch!!!

Friends need hugs!!

Not all my friends have just two legs. My tiniest one has four!

He's my dog, Hitch. He is absolutely the most lazy, laid back pooch in the world and I love him to bits.

His favourite activity is sleeping, followed by eating, then being hugged.

Normal walking is not his thing. He doesn't like pavements, his paws are too soft. So Mum has made him a carry-bag.

He stays all floppy, his skinny legs dangling from his carry-bag, with a bored look on his face… until we get to the park. Then he changes into

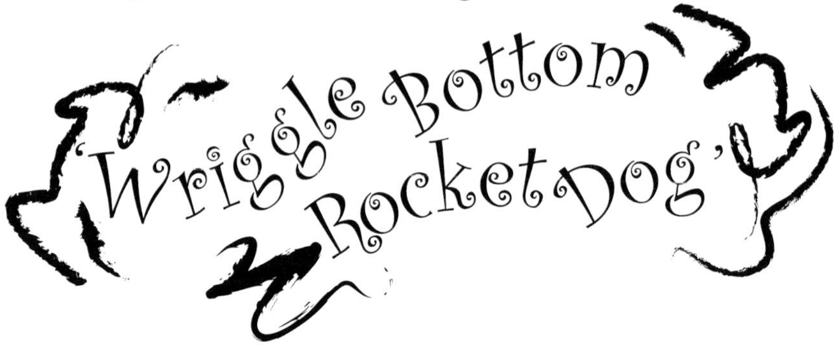

As soon as we walk through the gates he starts his 'park bark', goes all squirmy and tries to get out of his carry-bag.

Why? It's so simple. Squirrels!!!!! Or 'Grrrrrrrr….rrirrels' as Hitch calls them.

I don't know why he gets so trembly about them.

Most of the time they are hiding up the trees, but he does his 'zig-zag-squirrel-dance', from tree to tree running like a complete 'nutski'. I think he just wants to play with them, but I bet if he ever came face to face with one he would be totally scared. He's a

'Pathetic-pooch'!

Last week, Mum and I took him to the park. He was doing his usual squirrel dance when suddenly he stopped and let out a howl. We both ran very fast towards him. When we reached him, he was licking his paw and whimpering. Mum lifted his poorly paw and it was bleeding.

Some totally careless 'idiwit' had thrown a bottle on to the path and it was smashed into a zillion spikey shards. Hitch had cut his paw on a big pointy piece.

Mum was totally brill. She calmly picked Hitch up and tied her scarf round his paw to stop the bleeding. "Hurry up Nots, grab the carry bag. We must go straight to the vets."

We ran from the park and down the road towards the vets. Mum hugged Hitch tightly.

Our vet is Miss Valentine and she's lovely and kind.

She works at Paws and Claws Veterinary Clinic near our house.

Normally Hitch hates going to the vet but on this day he was all pathetic and limp. In reception, there was a very huge lady with the tiniest hamster popping out of her handbag.

Two children held a basket which was going "Meeow, meeow!" very loudly!

Meeow!!!

Meeow!!!

Meeow!!!

There was also a man with a ball of hair on the end of a lead.

I think it was a dog too.

The lady at the reception desk was very kind. When she saw the paw she said, "Oh dear, that looks nasty. I'll tell the vet immediately."

We were put at the front of the queue and in a very few minutes Miss Valentine came out and smiled. "Well, what has this young man been up to?"

As we walked into the surgery, Mum explained what had happened. Miss Valentine undid Mum's scarf and there was the bright red cut on Hitch's paw. A piece of sharp glass was still sticking out of it. I was feeling a bit sick, but I had

to be brave for Hitch.

She gave him an injection to stop it from hurting and soon removed the glass with her tweezers. "There, Hitch that's much better. Now let's get this cleaned up. I think you'll need a stitch or two."

She stitched up the cut in his foot just like Mum does when she sews a button on Dad's shirt.

Then she got something that looked like an upside-down lampshade and put it round Hitch's neck.

"This will stop him from nibbling his bandage," she said, smiling. "

I think the patient is well enough to go home."

Back home, we put Hitch on his dog bed and he looked **SOOOO** pathetic. I think he was totally embarrassed because of the lampshade thing round his neck.

He just lay on his bed all evening and wouldn't even eat his 'Dogotastic Munchy Mix'. He never misses supper because he's greedy.

Suddenly, I knew what he needed ~ a hug! I picked him up very gently, being careful not to hurt his paw and gave him a little hug. Not too squeezy, just right.

It's not easy hugging a dog that looks like a table lamp, but it worked. His little eyes lit up and he made the snuffly noise he makes when he's happy.

Miss Valentine is a wonderful vet, but a hug works every time.

Everybody needs a hug,
not just people
but cats and
dogs too!

...but not too tight.
We don't want
to squash them!

DOWN WITH MEAN

Down with mean!!

Specky-four-eyes!
Specasaurus!
Goggle Girl!
Window face!

These are just some of the totally mean and stupid names that 'idiwit' bullies call my friend Togs Fairway. Just because she wears specs!

She wears them because she has 'short-sighted' eyes. That means she can see things that are close up, but needs her specs to see things that are far away.

I think her specs make her look really intelligent and they're a real fashion statement.

When she takes them off, her face looks all empty. Togs isn't Togs without her specs.

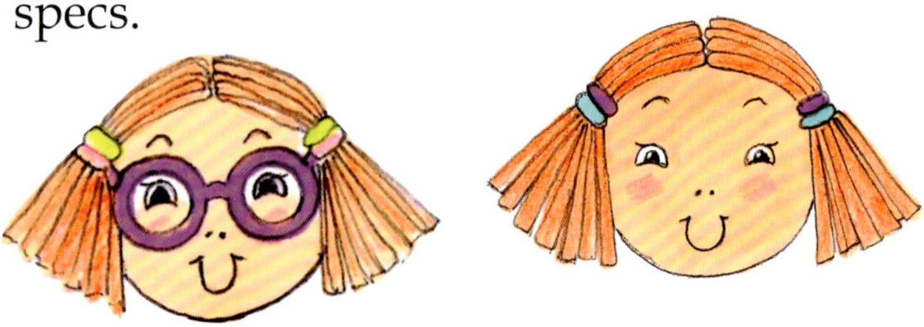

She's worn glasses for ever, so I got a huge surprise one day when I saw her walking towards me, spec-less!

I waved and waved but she didn't wave back. Why was she ignoring me?

Couldn't she **see** me?

That was it! No specs, no see! "Hi Togs! I'm over here, it's Nots! " I shouted.

She squeezed up her eyes and turned towards me. As she got closer, I could see her eyes were all red. In fact, she had been crying.

I ran towards her. "Togs, what's the matter, what's happened?"

She sobbed. "They… sniff…. broke… sniff…. my…. sniff… specs…. sniff!"

She reached into her school bag and pulled them out. Someone had cracked them in two, right across the middle.

I was sooo shocked. "Who did this?" I asked.

She was really blubbing now. "It's those big girls from Mrs Bucket's class. The ones that hang around the bus stop..."

I knew exactly who they were. Three cringey girls and the main one was called Hettie Hobble. Everyone said she had a mean mouth.

Togs wiped her eyes with a soggy tissue and continued. "They are totally 'uberstinky' and mean, just because I wear specs!"

She told me all the horrible names they called her, but today it had gone too far, they had snatched her specs right off her nose and smashed them.

Something had to be done to stop this, so I grabbed her arm and we ran towards our classroom. "We must tell Mrs Chippet right away. She'll know what to do."

Mrs Chippet is our teacher and she's simply 'wonderglorious'! We totally respect her. She has the smiliest face ~ except when we talk too much in class and then it gets 'splodie'.

She always knows what to do for the best.

Togs told her the whole story. She listened very carefully then dried Togs's tears. 'Leave it to me, I will sort it out."

She sent Togs home for the rest of the day and told me not to worry, all would be well. And it was.

I don't know what she said to horrible Hettie Hobble, but it did the trick.

PS. Can you help choose a new pair of specs for Togs? Find out how on page 100..........

No more nasty names
and no more broken specs.

Weeks later, I was walking home and there at the bus stop were Hettie and her horrid friends.

My tum did a flip-flop and I started to walk faster, then I noticed there was something really different about Hettie.

Perched on her nose was
a pair of bright blue specs!

I really wanted to say something 'sningey', but that would have made me mean too, so I just smiled and said, "Nice specs!"

I'm thinking there are too many bullies and meanies in the world and it makes me sad.

From people who bully and push people around at school, right up to the men who run countries and start horrid wars for stupid reasons. Bullies must be very unhappy people.

Wouldn't it be cool if we all stopped being mean and were just nice instead?

So, I've decided to do something about it. I'm just one little me, but this year I'm going to try really hard to make a difference to my world.

I know I can only do small things like being kind, helpful and patient, but if we all do just a few nice things, we can make a really big difference!

I'm going to start my own campaign.

'DOWN WITH MEAN!!'

Can you pick a new pair of specs for Togs?

Togs has lost her specs and her face looks empty. Can you pick a new pair and give her a totally new look? What will it be ~ glamorous... 'swotty'...or just plain Togs?

You choose....

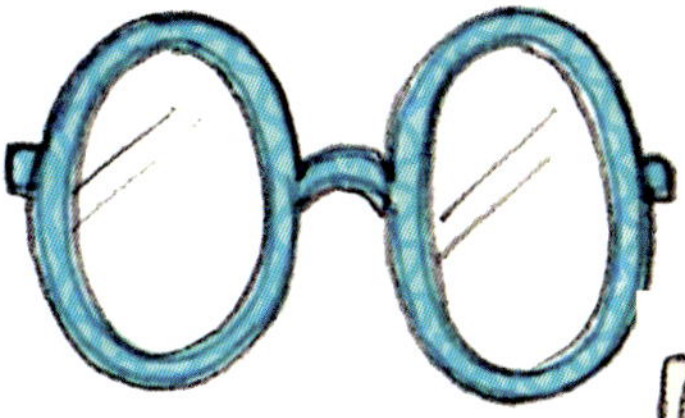

'Inky Swot'

'Glamour Puss'

'Career Girl'

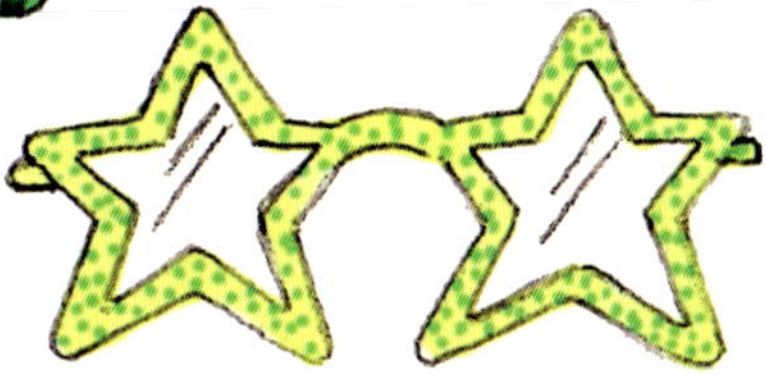

'Party Princess'

'Totally togs'

'Notstar Chic'

Natalie

Let's be friends!!

I think my brain needs a rest! It feels really 'tuzzled' like it's all full up!

I hope you liked my very first book. I'm loving sharing all my 'thinkings' and stories with you.

We girls (and boys) have got to stick together and work hard to make our world a really cool place to live in. I'm not a 'goody-two-shoes'

....sometimes even I can be 'scrinchy' ...but I do try very hard to be **kind and helpful** most of the time.

I think it's simple. It all starts with feeling good about just being you.

Love your talents and funny bits as well. It's fab that we all look so different and we're all good at different things too. It makes us individuals.

It also makes our world a really awesome place to live in.

Let's try very hard to love everyone and everything in our world. We can start with our family and 'besties' but we can all make a difference to the whole world if we just think about what we are doing and work hard to get things right.

It's not always easy to be nice when people are total 'bullies' or 'meanies' but I think they need help too.

They must be very unhappy people and we must never be mean to anyone.

Come and see me and Hitch on my website at **notalie.com**

There are loads of ideas for things to do and make and my blog too, so we can share our 'thinkings' together.

If you would like a 'fabaroonie' Notalie doll ~ nearly as tall as you are ~ you can find her on the website too!

And don't forget the cutest Hitch handbag, with a secret pocket in his tum.

Be happy, be helpful!

Love Notalie™ xxx

The best of friends.

Notaleese please!

Sometimes I get fuzzled and can't find the right word to say what I'm thinking about, so I just make up my own.

I **totally** love having my own language. I call it **Notalees**. This is my own dictionary of stuff...

Bling my thing ~ To light up and get **excited**

Blow my pooter ~ Losing my cool

Clompy ~ Stamping **hard** on the ground

Fabarooni ~ Really **good**

Fabolistic ~ Fabulous and fantastic squashed into one word

Fasholicious ~ Fashion that is totally delicious

Fuzzled ~ Confused

Grups ~ Grown ups

Idiwit ~ Someone who is reeeeally stupid

Irribabble ~ Irritating and annoying (like my big sister)

Knot ~ My closest bezzies

Knottled ~ Knotted up

Looperama ~ Crazy

Nutski ~ Someone who's loopy about something

Scrinchy ~ Bad tempered

Scrumerooni ~ Really tasty

Sningey ~ Someone mean and creepy

Splodie ~ Getting really **angry**

Superbulous ~ Something that's superb and fabulous at the same time

Tuzzy or tuzzled ~ Feeling **really** stuffed and full

Twingle ~ Twinge and tingle mixed together

Uberstinky ~ Really bad

Wibble ~ A wobble and a dribble all mixed up

Wonderglorious ~ Someone or something that is **totally wonderful**

BIG THANKS
to Joodle Doodle, Chuff
and Karen and big hugs
to Spud for letting me
stay up late to finish
the book.